IMAGES
of England

AROUND
ST ALBANS

Best wishes

Anne Wheeler

Tony Stevens

Dedication of the St Albans war memorial, 22 May 1921. With the war fresh in everyone's memory there was a huge response to the event. It is said that every family in the land lost someone close in the First World War. There are 640 people commemorated on the memorial, at least two St Albans families lost three sons and thirty-five lost two.

IMAGES
of England

AROUND
ST ALBANS

Compiled by
Anne Wheeler and Tony Stevens

ST ALBANS
MUSEUMS

TEMPUS

First published 2001
Copyright © Anne Wheeler and Tony Stevens, 2001

Tempus Publishing Limited
The Mill, Brimscombe Port,
Stroud, Gloucestershire, GL5 2QG

ISBN 0 7524 2289 8

Typesetting and origination by
Tempus Publishing Limited
Printed in Great Britain by
Midway Colour Print, Wiltshire

The Royal Engineers, Park Street Village, 1915. During the First World War the army would commandeer the resources it required including, in this case, the smithy. The blacksmith Herbert Martin (extreme right) had to train six soldiers as farriers. Herbert was shocked by the rough way they treated the horses and it is said that this made him decide to join the navy to fight his war. Herbert died in 1969 aged ninety-one. He was the last of a long line of blacksmiths to serve the village.

Contents

St Albans from the roof of the Abbey church, c. 1900. The view stretches from houses and shops on the High Street to St Peter's church in the distance. Behind the High Street, to the left of the Clock Tower, are the buildings of Dog Yard and Christopher Yard, on the site of what is now Christopher Place.

One
City Centre

St Peter's Street from the tower of St Peter's church, c. 1900. This rather unusual view illustrates just what an attractive street this must have been. It shows the avenue of lime trees, planted by Henry Gotto in 1881, particularly well.

London Road, looking towards the Peahen crossroads, *c.* 1905. The Cross Keys pub can be seen on the corner of Chequer Street. Next to it is Hudson's cycle shop and on the other side of the road is the Public Benefit Boot Company. The tower on the corner of High Street and Chequer Street has since been demolished.

High Street, looking towards the Peahen crossroads, *c.* 1925. By the 1920s we see open-topped motor cars rather than horses and carts. High Street shops included the Home and Colonial Stores, Dorrells and Lyons Tea Rooms. The fountain, designed by George Gilbert Scott and paid for by Mrs Isabella Worley was located here from 1872 until the late 1920s.

St Albans Town Hall, *c.* 1890. St Albans is a market town and until the 1970s animals were bought and sold in the city centre every Wednesday. The livestock market is often associated with cattle but here we see a trader arriving with sheep on a wet winter's morning.

The general market, *c.* 1905. St Peter's Street on a Saturday is viewed from the balcony of the Town Hall. The covered market stalls in the foreground include W. Seamons & Son Fruit and Flower Growers of Dunstable.

The cattle market, *c*. 1905. The weekly cattle market was an important local event. It was also a popular spectator sport with local children.

The cattle market, *c*. 1915. Here cattle can be seen tethered to the railings rather than penned in. The London and County Bank (now Nat West) is clearly visible. In 1926 the livestock market was moved to premises in Drovers Way.

The Saturday market, c. 1905. From the balcony of the Town Hall, this view along St Peter's Street shows just how wide the service road really is. The water trough for horses was outside the Town Hall until the mid-1920s.

St Peter's Street, c. 1905. The only traffic here is either horse-drawn or people-powered. A large statue of an angel marks the Angel Boot Stores. It is said to have come from the Angel Inn in Verulam Road which closed around 1890.

The Town Hall and Market Place, c. 1905. Market day was obviously a popular day to take photographs! Each gas lamp had to be lit individually, hence the ladder.

Cells beneath the Town Hall, 1979. The Town Hall, built in 1831, was originally also the Court House. Under the court is a series of cells where prisoners were kept immediately before and after their trial. This photograph, from long after they were last used, provides a gloomy insight into nineteenth-century law and order.

The No. 84 bus in St Peter's Street, *c.* 1913. Bound for Golders Green station, the open-topped No. 84 bus carries adverts for Wood Milne who made rubber tyres and rubber heels and tips. Pocock's Dairy is on the corner of Waddington Road and the White Horse pub is next door but one.

St Peter's Street, late 1920s. By 1930 motor transport was the way to travel! The bus is still open-topped but the cars have canvas tops which could be pulled over in case of rain. J. Sainsbury's shop is clearly visible; next door but one is Page and Son's furniture repository (now Woolworth's).

The clock tower, c. 1871. Before 1872 when Isabella Worley's water fountain was constructed, an iron water pump adorned the site. It was of ornate design and combined a gas lamp as well as the pump. The posters around the railings advertise Easter holiday outings to London on the Midland Railway.

Market stall at the foot of the clock tower during the 1880s. For many years there was a stall selling fruit and vegetables here.

Looking up Holywell Hill, *c.* 1875. The un-restored abbey is visible behind the Duke of Marlborough pub. At this time the pub was selling ales by Lattimore's Brewery of Wheathampstead as well as Burton Ales.

Looking down Holywell Hill, *c.* 1910. Deayton's grocery stores can be seen to the right of the photograph.

Ivy House, No. 107 St Peter's Street, during the 1920s. Photographed from St Peter's churchyard it is easy to see why Ivy House is so called. It was built and used by Edward Strong, Master Mason, who is famous for his work on St Paul's Cathedral, London. He died in 1723 and is buried at St Peter's church where there is a memorial to him.

Detail above the doorway of Ivy House, c. 1970. These symbols, which are thought to be Masonic in origin, were probably designed by Edward Strong. Strong was a founder of Freemasonry and St Alban is the patron saint of Freemasons.

Two

The Rural City

Verulam Hills farm, *c.* 1900. The farm buildings and haystacks are overlooked by the recently restored abbey. The buildings have been demolished and the land is now part of Verulamium Park.

St Albans from the south east during the 1880s. The St Albans to Watford railway can be seen between the lines of fencing cutting across the centre of the picture. The railway opened in 1858.

Summertime, c. 1905. Women and children sit amongst the hay in poses that were typical of the time. The image of the romantic rural idyll is less to do with the lifestyle of the people as to the need to sit still for the long exposures required by the camera.

Bringing in the harvest, *c.* 1900. James Eaton Hammond, tenant farmer of St Germain's farm brings in the harvest with the aid of his workers and helpers. The string around the trouser legs was intended to protect the wearer from terrified mice running up them in a panic.

Mechanised reaping, St Germain's farm, *c.* 1900. In 1929 the owner of St Germain's farm, the Earl of Verulam, sold the farm to the City Corporation. It now forms the greater part of Verulamium Park.

Watercress beds, Park Street, *c*. 1950. Between the wars the Pinnock family dominated the local business with beds along the Ver Valley in Bricket Wood, Frogmore, Park Street, on land either side of Holywell Hill, Gorhambury Drive and Codicote. They generated so much rail freight traffic that the Abbey Flyer line became known locally as 'The Watercress Line'.

Javeleau's workshop, Fishpool Street, 1962. Javeleau's operated a Rustic Garden Furniture business from this site. This road, with dilapidated cottages and run down businesses was once considered one of the least desirable places to live. Originally on the coach route to the north west, many of its buildings are now restored and listed, making this an attractive and upmarket street.

The River Ver, c. 1906. In common with all rivers, the Ver is a magnet for walkers. For generations, families have strolled along the peaceful banks, diverted and amused by the abundant wildlife. This photograph is from the time before St Germain's farm was sold, as evidenced by the cattle grazing in the field and the absence of the ornamental lakes.

Building the ornamental lakes, Verulamium Park, 1929. Unemployed labourers from the north of England helped construct the lakes. They provide a haven for water birds and one of the islands supports a well-established heronry.

Women farm workers, *c.* 1920. Helen Peacock (left) was in the Women's Land Army during the First World War. At the time of this photograph she was working on a farm on the Redbourn Road, St Albans.

The Marshalswick estate under construction, 1959. As the demand for housing increased after the Second World War farmers and landowners found the sale of their acres was profitable. This trend continued with the adjacent development of the Jersey Farm estate in the 1980s. Sandpit Lane is visible in the foreground with Barnfield Road leading to The Ridgeway.

Three

The Villages

Colney Heath, c. 1905. When photography was still a novelty it was good business to photograph familiar streets and panoramas and to sell the images on postcards. These were popular with residents and visitors alike. Thus it is possible that somewhere there exists a photograph of every village in the land. The house on the right appears in the next photograph.

Mr Nash and the Bush family, Colney Heath, *c*. 1900. Here the Bush family stand proudly outside their detached house in Colney Heath.

The Swains, Colney Heath, *c*. 1897. Gathered together for a family celebration, probably a wedding, Mr and Mrs Swain (Lucy) with sons, daughters and a niece (the youngest girl) are stiff and formal in their 'Sunday best'. The cottage probably stood near the Crooked Billet Inn.

Hawkswick, Harpenden Road, c. 1900. With its own private gasworks, Hawkswick is located on the outskirts of St Albans, near Childwickbury. Such houses attracted wealthy residents including Sir Blundell Maple of Maples furnishing fame and the reclusive film director, Stanley Kubrick.

Harpenden, c. 1900. Although Harpenden is now a town, residents still refer to the centre as 'The Village' because of its extensive green spaces and open common land. This photograph is from when Harpenden really was a village. The cart stands in front of The Red Lion pub.

Nomansland Common, 1952. Used for recreation by local people the common is sometimes also used by travellers. In past times they supplied farmers with cheap casual labour but a revolution in mechanised farming has denied travellers this source of income. This photograph provided evidence for an eviction order.

Town Farm, Wheathampstead, c. 1885. Occupied by the Chennells family, this farm was situated on the corner of The Hill and Marford Road. Formerly known as Chennells Farm this 400-year-old building was demolished without planning permission leading to a major court case. A row of terraced houses has now been built on the site.

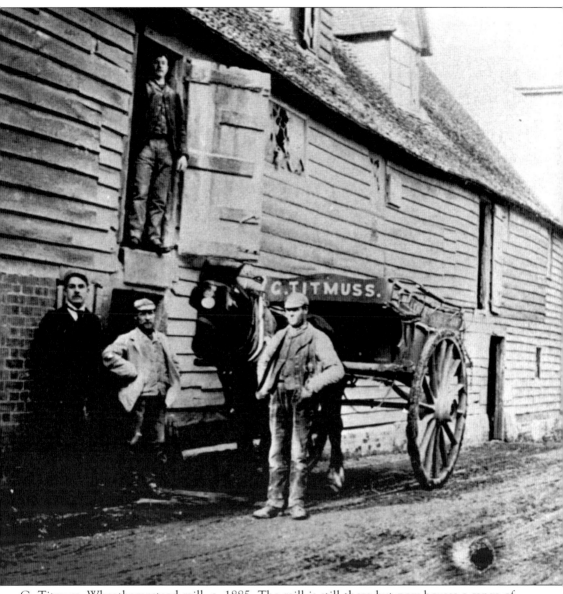

G. Titmuss, Wheathampstead mill, *c.* 1885. The mill is still there but now houses a range of retail shops. G.J.W. Titmuss Ltd is still working out of Wheathampstead and now produces pet foods.

St Michael's village in the snow, *c*. 1965. Heavy snowfalls were a regular event for a major part of the twentieth century but climate change has meant that in this part of England sights such as this are increasingly rare. The barn in the foreground has been demolished to enlarge the car park of the Rose and Crown pub.

St Germain's farmhouse, St Michael's village, *c*. 1910. The farm was situated where Verulamium Park is today. Since 1939 Verulamium Museum has stood on the ground once occupied by the house. The museum was built to house many of the items found by Sir Mortimer Wheeler and his team of archaeologists during the excavations of the 1930s.

Mrs Ellen Holland-Hibbert and children, c. 1892. Mrs Holland-Hibbert, seen here with daughter Elsie and son Thurston, was the wife of the 3rd Viscount Knutsford of Munden. The Holland-Hibbert family can trace their history at Munden House, Bricket Wood back 394 years. As a consequence of the Victorian and Edwardian fashions for dressing pre-school children the same way young boys often wore dresses.

BRICKET WOOD COMMON.

Bricket Wood Common, c. 1910. The wooded area of the common used to be coppiced before the Second World War and cattle were grazed on the land. Parts of this are ancient woodland and rare and scientifically interesting plants have been found here. For that reason significant parts of the common are designated as sites of special scientific interest.

Redbourn war memorial, 13 June 1920. Scenes such as this were repeated in the villages surrounding St Albans. The Cornish granite obelisk is inscribed with the names of fifty-seven local men who lost their lives in the First World War. The Marquess of Salisbury unveiled the memorial.

The Bull, Redbourn, c. 1900. An important inn on the route taken by heavy coaches to the North West, at one time it had stabling for eighty horses. First mentioned in 1595, it tried to keep up with the times. The sign on the wall next to the wrought iron bracket reads, 'Head Quarters of the Bicycle Touring Club.' The extravagantly ornate bracket was removed in 1902.

32

Steetley chemicals, Sandridge, 1973. The factory in House Lane opened in 1955 as an Ethyl Bromide plant. This hazardous chemical was used in pesticides and as a refrigerant. The facility closed in the late 1970s and the site has since been developed as St Leonard's Court.

The Three Horseshoes, Smallford, c. 1920. First recorded in 1735 the inn was located on a turnpike road. The name derives from the association with blacksmiths' premises, often to be found next to inns. While the horse that had lost its shoe was being re-shod the travellers could refresh themselves in the adjacent hostelry. The pub is still there today.

London Colney, *c.* 1955. The village of London Colney was on the coaching route from London and once boasted twenty-six inns. The area around the River Colne forms the historic heart of the village. The Swan pub on the right has long since closed.

The River Ver, Park Street, *c.* 1945. Park Street is an old farming village subject to ribbon development and industrialisation, but still an attractive rural place to live. Behind Park Street and Frogmore villages are restored gravel pits, much favoured by walkers and fishermen. Over the road, the River Ver is flanked by old watercress beds and river meadows.

Four
Verulamium

Uncovering mosaics, Verulamium, 1930s. The Wheelers uncovered and recorded some of the fine town houses at Verulamium. These often had decorative mosaic floors such as the 'Chequerboard' Mosaic shown here.

Excavations in the Revd Bicknell's garden, 1911. Bicknell was the vicar of St Michael's church and was also a keen amateur archaeologist. This is the earliest photograph of a dig at Verulamium.

Photographing the finds, Verulamium, 1930s. Mortimer Wheeler oversees the photography of excavated features in the 1930s. Wheeler was one of the first archaeologists to recognize the value of photography as a recording medium.

Lunchtime during the Wheeler excavations, Verulamium, 1930s.

Excavations, Bluehouse Hill, *c*. 1960. During the 1950s and 1960s a second phase of excavations was carried out at Verulamium along the route of the soon to be constructed Bluehouse Hill. Note the personalised wheelbarrow to the right.

Cleaning and recording, Bluehouse Hill, *c.* 1960. These excavations along the route of Bluehouse Hill were supervised by Professor Sheppard Frere. A number of new mosaics were discovered that required detailed cleaning and recording.

Five

Fleetville

Hatfield Road, 1903. Hatfield Road was no more than a country lane bordered by fields and trees at the time of this photograph. A mother and children happily walk down the middle of the road. The arrival of Smiths' Printing Agency in 1898 heralded the start of the development of the area and transformed it from open countryside to a thriving new industrial and residential area.

P.H. Stone, wine and spirit merchant, Hatfield Road, 1902. This off-licence stood on the corner of Sutton Road where the Rat's Castle pub now stands. Before this, a toll house for the Reading and Hatfield Turnpike Trust occupied the site.

Smiths' Printing Agency, Hatfield Road, c. 1900. Smiths' came to St Albans from the Fleet Street area of London seeking clean air and willing employees for its expanding business. The building was called Fleet Works and it is from this that Fleetville gets its name. The company was responsible for building roads, houses and shops around the factory.

Aerial view of the site of Smiths' printers, c. 1950. At the time of this photograph the building was occupied by the Ballito Hosiery mills. Marconi Instruments later used the building to the rear of the site and Laver's timber yard was adjacent. Behind the railway line caravans provided temporary accommodation.

Munitions workers, Ballito Hosiery mills, 1944. During the Second World War workers at the factory switched from making stockings to making munitions, particularly Oerlikon shells.

Arthur Road, decorated to celebrate the Silver Jubilee of King George V, 1935. This was one of several roads built by Smiths' to house their workers. The taller building on the left hand corner was the Fleetville Institute which comprised a concert room, reading and smoke rooms, gymnasium and billiard room.

Bycullah Terrace, Hatfield Road, *c.* 1905. This parade opposite Smiths' was originally built to house the managers. It soon provided shops and cafés as well as houses. The Terrace was named *Bycullah* (a place in India) after Mr Smith's house in London.

Beaumont works, Sutton Road, *c.* 1903. This very ornate factory was built for Nicholson & Co., coat manufacturers, in 1900. The business was started by Alfred J. Nicholson in Manchester in 1891 and moved to St Albans to be nearer his London customers. The building appears to be quite isolated – Sutton Road is a muddy track with fields beyond.

Interior of Nicholson's factory during the 1930s. This work room is festooned with Christmas decorations and the calendar on the wall reads 2 January. In the 1930s a department specialising in making mackintoshes and other waterproofs was opened. The factory closed in the 1970s but the building remains.

Aerial view of the extended Nicholson's factory, c. 1925/30. The works were extended many times between 1900 and 1950 and the workforce grew from 40 to 200. Hedley Road had just been laid out but no houses had yet been built.

Flooding under the Sutton Road railway bridge, 1910. The road under the railway bridge used to flood on a fairly regular basis during the early twentieth century – hence the title of this photograph *The River Sutton*. It became a popular place with children who enjoyed paddling and swimming here.

Six

Industry

Hucks Starters, Park Street, *c*. 1922. These very unusual vehicles relate to the prominent local industry of aircraft manufacture. Known as Hucks Starters, the vehicles were made by the Park Street firm of Hayter and Thomas and were used to start the engines of early aircraft.

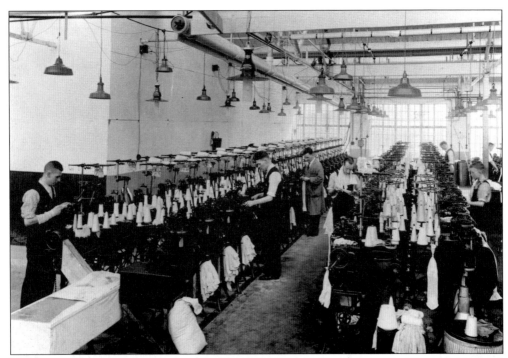

Making stockings, Ballito Hosiery mills, Fleetville, 1939. Ballito came to St Albans in 1925 and by the 1950s employed over 1,000 people. Special machines were imported from America and Ballito became the first company in the country to mass produce silk stockings.

Packaging for Ballito 'Pinpoint' stockings, 1950s. A whole range of stockings in both silk and nylon were produced at the factory in Hatfield Road. The company supplied Marks & Spencer and it was the withdrawal of this contract that contributed to the closure of the firm in 1967.

The boiler house, Ballito Hosiery mills, 1944. The everyday maintenance of a factory is obviously of prime importance, but can also be an aspect of factory life which often goes unrecorded. Here we see staff maintaining the boiler which provided heat and power throughout the factory.

Munitions workers, Ballito Hosiery mills, 1944. During the Second World War, numerous local women worked at Ballito making Oerlikon shells. The work was very dangerous and involved live ammunition. These women are packing the projectiles for the finished shells.

Demonstration by Marconi Instruments, *c.* 1950. Marconi came to St Albans in 1941 and in 1946 the company acquired a site at Longacres which became its headquarters. Marconi was a major local employer with over 3,000 employees in its heyday. The company left St Albans in 1995 and the site has been developed as housing.

Brooke Bond factory, Redbourn, *c.* 1950s. Brooke Bond came to Redbourn in 1940. During the Second World War cocoa was packed on this site. Later tea and coffee were also processed and packaged at the Redbourn factory. The factory closed in 1993 and most of the site is now housing. Redbourn Village Museum occupies another part of the site.

The sewing room, Lees' Boot and Shoe factory, 1927. Lees' factory was in Grosvenor Road from 1893, until the 1950s when the business closed. The company made ladies' and children's shoes until the 1940s, at which time they decided to concentrate on the manufacture of ladies' footwear and stopped producing shoes for children.

The machine room, Lees' Boot and Shoe factory, 1927. Here we see the shoes nearing completion. Edwin Lee, the founder of the company, was Mayor of St Albans in 1903.

Co-op dairy, Fleetville, *c.* 1950. The Co-op dairy in Burleigh Road opened in 1933 and is still there to this day. Churns, instead of the now familiar milk bottles, were used to collect milk from local farms.

The old Kingsbury Brewery, Verulam Road, 1964. This building still stands near the corner of Branch Road. It was one of five breweries operating in St Albans in the mid-nineteenth century. The last one to close was Adey and White's (where the Maltings Shopping Centre is now situated) which was taken over by Green's of Luton in 1936 and closed a few months later.

The gas works, Holywell Hill, *c*. 1955. The gas works dominated the area by the Abbey Station at the bottom of Holywell Hill. This clever view juxtaposes the serenity of the abbey with the 'smog' of the gas works. It was demolished in the early 1970s and offices, shops and car parks now occupy most of the site.

J. Charkham, salvage merchant, *c*. 1950. Between the gas works and the Abbey Station there was a scrap yard run by J. Charkham. It was based at this site from 1940 to 1958.

Young straw-plaiters, c. 1910. Unfortunately we do not know anything about these particular little girls busily plaiting straw; but straw plaiting was a very important local industry employing thousands of women and children. Straw was usually plaited in the home and then sold to hat manufacturers through the market.

Making straw hats, *c*. 1920. During the 1880s many large purpose-built hat factories were constructed around the junction of Victoria Street and Marlborough Road. This area became the epicentre of the local hat industry. By 1930 most of the factories had closed due to foreign competition and changes in fashion.

H.P. Smith's hat factory, Victoria Street, late 1920s. Henry Partridge Smith's factory was in the heart of the straw hat area and was on the site of the present job centre. Grace Butterfield (later Fitzjohn) was the forelady of the factory and can be seen on the left of this photograph.

Moor Mill, near St. Albans.

Moor Mill, Bricket Wood, *c.* 1910. This mill, situated on the River Ver, was built in 1762 and replaced a much earlier one. It operated as a flour mill until 1939 after which the building fell into disrepair. In 1992 it was restored and is now a restaurant.

The Silk Mill, Abbey Mill Lane, *c.* 1900. On the site of the medieval Abbey Corn Mills, the Silk Mill is situated on the River Ver opposite the Fighting Cocks pub. Between 1804 and 1905 it was owned by the Woollam family and many children were employed there. It continued as a working mill until 1938.

Seven

Shops

F. Blanks, wine and spirit merchant, and Oakley's butchers, Lattimore Road, *c.* 1890. Situated near the junction with London Road, there was a butcher's shop here until around 2000 when the building was converted into a house.

Wiles and Lewis, candle manufacturers, George Street, *c.* 1885. This building on the corner of Verulam Road is now the Tudor Tavern. The tallow works was moved to Bernards Heath in 1886 following numerous complaints about the offensive smell coming from the premises.

R.E. Holdham's butchers, Park Street, 1932. In this photograph, by Cherry of St Albans, we see butcher and one time Mayor of St Albans (1949), Ralph Holdham, standing proudly outside his shop. It was quite usual for butchers to 'dress' their shops in this very elaborate way at this time.

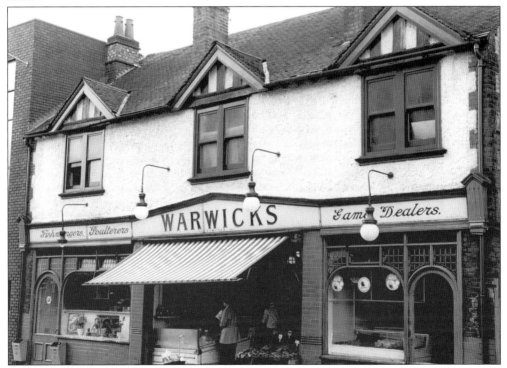

Warwick's fish shop, Catherine Street, 1984. The Warwick family ran a chain of shops in St Albans from the 1920s to the 1980s. Although locally known as 'fish shops', they also sold poultry and game. In 1997 St Albans Museums acquired a 1930s 'Warwick's' crisp packet. Frederick Warwick was Mayor of St Albans in 1933.

W. Gibbons, boot maker, Harpenden, *c.* 1905. An advert for this shop in the 1902 St Albans Directory states that W. Gibbons, 'having had fourteen years London experience, can compete with London Houses, both as to style and durability'. All kinds of boots could be made to order at three days notice. The shop was on Leyton Road, opposite Anscombes (now Waitrose).

Oggelsby's motor and cycle works, Harpenden, 1908. This shop in Southdown Road obviously sold prams as well as bicycles. It also advertises shoeing and general smithy work. As the century progressed the Oggelsby family moved more and more towards selling motor cars. There is still an Oggelsby's garage in Harpenden today.

B.A. Tuckett's general store, No. 213 Camp Road, during the 1930s. Judging from the window and doorway displays this shop appears to sell just about everything! It also boasts the lowest prices.

Arthur Payne's second-hand furniture shop, Victoria Street, c. 1960. This was one of several second-hand furniture shops in Victoria Street in the 1950s and 1960s. The lady here is Audrey Wadowska, daughter of local film pioneer Arthur Melbourne-Cooper.

Milk cart, 1924. William Petersen had a milk delivery business based in Sopwell Lane. He used to do three rounds a day – the 'breakfast' the 'pudding' and the 'tea' – starting at 5.00 a.m. and finishing at 4.30 p.m. Milk was sold direct from the churn using pint and half-pint measures. He is pictured in Sopwell Lane with his three-wheeled hand-cart.

Delivery cart, Steer's family butcher, during the 1920s. Mr E.H. Steer had a butcher's shop at No. 23 Chequer Street during the 1920s. As was usual with many shops at the time, produce was also delivered door to door. Here we see the cart in Hall Place Gardens, looking over towards Townsend Avenue and the St Albans High School for Girls.

St Peter's Street, *c.* 1945. By the late 1930s large chain stores such as Marks & Spencer, True-Form, Woolworth's, Home and Colonial and Sainsbury's had shops in St Peter's Street. Also seen here are Meaker's Outfitters, W.R. Kingham's tobacconists and the Foot Clinic which was accessed through the True-Form shoe shop.

St Albans British workman's coffee tavern, French Row, *c.* 1900. Connected with the Temperance movement of the period, the coffee tavern was basically an alcohol-free pub. Established in 1879, it was a public company, with 100 shares priced at £1 each. Directors of the tavern included H.J. Toulmin (mayor) and Richard Gibbs of Gibbs and Bamforth.

Wedge's shop, No. 12 Verulam Road, 1974. Violet Wedge ran a ships' chandler's shop in St Albans for nearly fifty years. She was based at this shop until 1982 when it was demolished to make way for the Christopher Place Shopping Centre. After a 'battle' with the developers she moved across the road where she traded until her death in 1989 at the age of eighty-eight.

Tesco, No. 67a St Peter's Street, 1962. This Tesco was the first self-service supermarket in the country. For many years in the 1970s and 1980s, clothes, toys and homewares were sold on the first floor. The shop was extended next door to the building that had been Butler's butchers shortly after this picture was taken.

Eight

Transport

London Road station, 1867. This station, part of the Hatfield to St Albans branch of the Great Northern Railway, opened in 1865. The line was closed in the 1960s and the station was taken over by a business dealing in army surplus vehicles. Now part of a housing development, the station has been converted into offices.

Bridge over the Hatfield to St Albans branch line, 1867. A contractor's locomotive with an open cab is pictured on the soon to be opened London Midland Railway. The line below is the St Albans to Hatfield branch line, now the Alban Way footpath and cycleway.

London Road bridge, 1867. In 1868 the main line from St Albans City to London was opened dealing the final blow to the remnants of the coaching trade. The new bridge is getting its final coat of paint here and in the distance the old London Road tollgate and house awaits its doom. The tollgate finally closed in 1871.

Victoria Street, *c*. 1905. Not a car or bus in sight as passengers walk home from St Albans city station. The lady wheeling the bicycle on the right is an early indication of women's increasing liberation from strict Victorian convention.

Jim Selby, coachman, 1860. Jim Selby drove a coach to Brighton and back in seven hours and thirty-four minutes for a £1,000 wager; which he won. He is dressed in typical coachman's uniform of the time.

Regulator coach outside the Peahen Inn, c. 1897. St Albans was a major coaching centre with up to 1,400 horses stabled in the town; catering for six- and four-horse teams. The noise and smell must have been considerable. Due to the rapid expansion of rail travel from 1838 to 1880, the coaching industry declined and eventually vanished.

Abbey station, *c.* 1955. The Abbey station originally had eight bays. As traffic declined it was reduced to five bays, and the buildings were finally demolished in the 1970s. The station is now an unmanned single-bay operation with fares collected by a 'conductor' on the train.

Waiting room, Ayot station, *c.* 1950. The drab gentility of a station waiting room, frequently reserved for women only, is now just a memory. The small hatch to the left is where tickets were sold.

The Earl of Verulam's steamer, *c.* 1900. Early cars were often driven by steam, not much of a problem when staff carried out the lengthy process of getting up steam. The petrol engine was more responsive but steam remained as a competitor until the petrol engine and the supply of its fuel achieved a higher degree of reliability.

Ver garage, *c.* 1920. Ver Garage is situated at the foot of Holywell Hill and is still there today although with a very different appearance. Whatever happened to Redline Petrol?

Bus, *c.* 1925. This bus, operated by the District Company, ran to St Albans Market Place via the LMS station. There was a time when the engines did not have enough power to take buses up Holywell Hill. A traction engine was available to tow vehicles up the hill when needed.

Motorcyclists, Great Red Lion Hotel, *c.* 1910. A group of motorcyclists line up for a portrait outside the garage of the Great Red Lion in Verulam Road. Was this early motorcycle club, the Edwardian equivalent of the Hells Angels?

Butler's, butchers, delivery cart, c. 1910. E. Butler had several butcher's shops in the district, one of the best-known being on the site now occupied by Tesco. They had a number of horse and trap units that were used to deliver the meat. It was sometimes difficult to persuade the horse to park parallel to the kerb.

Smith's cleaners delivery van, c. 1920. Many small traders, particularly those serving rural communities, did not miss the commercial opportunities offered by the delivery van. Transport times were reduced and greater distances could be covered. This was particularly important when the great majority of their customers had no cars of their own.

Clerics with bikes, *c.* 1905. Two ecclesiastical gentlemen have chosen a bike as a posing aid, a device much favoured by Edwardian photographers. The bicycle is interesting because, despite the un-metalled state of many roads of the time, there is no front mudguard. The state of the front tyre shows that there was plenty of mud about.

Adams' van, St Peter's Street, *c.* 1900. Commercial vehicles had to be reliable and steam technology was well established by the start of the twentieth century. The fuel for these vehicles was also easily available. This van clearly owes its lineage to the traction engines widely used in agriculture at the time.

Handley Page HP42 Hadrian, June 1931. Built at Colney Street this was one of eight of the most elegant bi-planes ever built. Four aircraft were based at Cairo and the remaining four based at Croydon. The figure under the wing is the engineer from the Bristol Engine Company, who was the boyfriend of the Park Street girl who took this photograph.

City of St Albans Spitfire, 1942. During the Second World War there were appeals for money and scrap materials to help the war effort. The government encouraged civic participation by naming ships and aircraft after the contributor city. There was a destroyer called HMS *St Albans*. The practice continued after the war with a steam locomotive called *City of St Albans*.

Nine
Education

Alma Road School, 1913. This school, on the corner of Bedford Road, was for girls and infants during 1913. It appears that the girls have recently been studying wildlife and their work is decorating one of the classroom walls. The other wall stores numerous dumbbells for use in PT classes.

Procession to lay the foundation stone at St Albans Grammar School, 1907. It is interesting to note that this is described as a Masonic procession. The school obviously has fairly close links with the Freemasons, as the keystone to a later extension was laid with full Masonic honours. From this angle a good view of the High Street can be seen.

The abbey gateway, c. 1900. The great gateway was purchased by the governors of St Albans School in 1871 and housed the whole school until 1908 when the new school was built next door. Prior to this, the gateway was used as a prison and the Lady Chapel in the abbey was used as the school.

The High School, St. Albans,

St Albans High School for Girls, *c.* 1912. Situated on Townsend Avenue, this shows the purpose-built school shortly after its completion. At this time there were 160 scholars under the supervision of the headmistress, Miss H.A. Ashworth, nine assistant mistresses and three visiting teachers.

The science lab, St Albans Boys' Modern School, 1938. This is one of a series of photographs promoting the newly built school on Brampton Road. Described at the time as 'one of the finest examples of school architecture in the Country', it has had various names over the years and is now known as Verulam School.

Girls' houses, National Children's Home, Harpenden, c. 1915. The National Children's Home and Orphanage was built in Ambrose Lane in 1910. On the same site there was a sanatorium for children with consumption.

The gift house, National Children's Home, Harpenden, c. 1915. Smartly dressed boys wearing Eton collars pose for a group photograph outside one of the buildings. The buildings remain and are known as the Highfield Oval. Youth with a Mission are now based at the site.

The printing works, National Children's Home, Harpenden, c. 1915. The home was well equipped and had its own printing works where children (boys) could learn a trade to prepare them for independent adult life.

The craft workshop, National Children's Home, Harpenden, c. 1920s. Boys were also taught woodworking skills. Girls tended to be taught domestic skills such as cooking and cleaning to prepare them for a life in service.

Children from Bernards Heath Infants School, *c.* 1910. These young children are dressed up for a performance at the Culver Road Hall. Unfortunately we don't know the occasion, perhaps it was to celebrate Empire Day or maybe the coronation of King George V in 1911?

Children from Redbourn Infants School, 1930s. The school buildings on East Common can be seen in the background.

Empire Day, Hatfield Road Boys School, 1912. This school was on the site of the present College of Law, and parts of the building still remain. With 395 boys in attendance in 1912, it was one of the biggest schools in St Albans. School leaving age was thirteen at this time.

Camp Schools, *c.* 1916. Opened in 1898, the building comprised an infant school and a mixed junior school. They each had their own head teacher and staff. For many years Mr Wimbury ran the juniors and his wife ran the infants. Here a group of First World War soldiers stand outside the school.

ST. ALBANS ADULT SCHOOL.
Annual Outing to Aldenham, Aug. 26th, 1911.

St Albans adult school outing, 1911. The adult school met on Sundays at premises in Upper Lattimore Road until 1912 when a new adult school was built on the corner of Stanhope Road and Granville Road. Although the school was open to men and women, only men appear in this photograph.

Ten
Sport and Leisure

St Albans High School for Girls sports day, *c*. 1910. An early example of the 'action shot'. Taken for granted in modern sports photography, this frozen moment in time was much more of an achievement with the equipment then available. How would a modern female athlete take to competing encumbered with a long skirt like this?

The first day of the Odeon kids club, Grand Palace cinema, 15 May 1943. Who can forget the 'Saturday Morning Pictures'? There was the sing-song accompanied by the cinema organ, with the ball bouncing along the words on the screen and the cartoon and comedy film followed by the main feature – typically a Roy Rogers cowboy epic.

George Willett, projectionist at the Odeon, 1960s. George recalls his time at the cinema: 'We often used to have packed houses and we used to seat 1,600 people – 1,000 downstairs in the stalls and 600 in the circle. If it was good comedy on, we used to go out and sit in the auditorium to get the atmosphere of it.'

Popsey Dorling, usherette, Odeon cinema, 1948-1969. *Popsey remembers that:* In those days the sales kept the cinemas going, they were very important. That's on a Saturday morning and we used to have 'Popsey's Popcorn' would you believe. That's a picture of me selling it there.

Head steward of Batchwood Hall, c. 1970. Don Brewer, the steward was moving to Leeds. In appreciation of past services the captain of Batchwood Golf club presented him with a leather wallet and a cheque from the club members.

Batchwood Hall, c. 1960. One time home to Sir Edmund Beckett, 1st Baron Grimthorpe, it was purchased by St Albans City Council in 1935 for use as a restaurant and eighteen-hole municipal golf course. The restaurant is now a nightclub and the golf course is increasingly popular, providing public access without having to pay for membership and exclusivity.

Ice cream van, Bricket Wood Fair, *c.* 1925. We are all familiar with the mobile ice cream sellers and their amplified jingles. This early version had no fewer than three staff involved in its operation, typical of the manpower intensive services of the day.

Boating, St Michael's Manor, *c.* 1920. This boat is on the fish pond in the grounds of St Michael's Manor hotel, Fishpool Street. The boat was provided for the pleasure of the guests.

Cricketer, *c.* 1890. Cricket was always a favourite rural sport in England. This member of the Bush family of Colney Heath strikes a noble pose in full kit against an incongruous neo-classical background.

Firemen at Park Street sports, *c.* 1890. There is a long tradition of fire service displays at village events, both to promote a fire prevention message and in the early years to raise money. Large factories, insurance companies and sometimes cities, funded fire brigades. Funding was rarely adequate and displays were used as a means of encouraging sponsorship and other donations.

Cricket team, *c.* 1900. This team had managed to purchase a team cap but little else. They have their own scorer (cross-legged, at the front, left) and umpire (standing far right). The bowler-hat brigade at the back were presumably the team sponsors.

Bernards Heath Junior League, 1929. The Bernards Heath School team poses proudly with their Junior League Championship trophy, the Debenham shield.

Sixth-form pupils, Verulam Boys' School, c. 1955. The starting gun has been fired and these athletes surge away from the start all wearing very intense expressions.

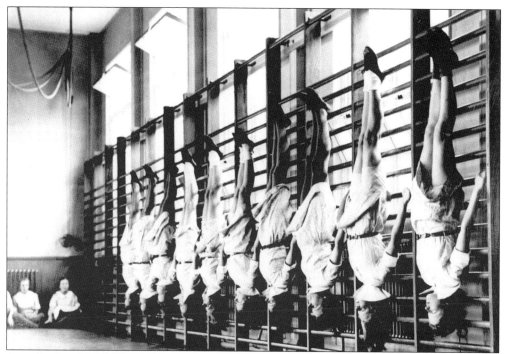

Gym display, St Albans High School for Girls, 1937. A gym display is captured on film for the pleasure of parents and the enduring embarrassment of the pupils. Little did they know that in three short years most of them would be called to do their bit for the war effort.

Lacrosse stick practice, St Albans High School for Girls, 1927. This game is associated in people's minds with the private school system. Originally played as training for warfare by Native Americans it was introduced to Britain in 1867. The women's world championship was first held in 1969 and was won by Great Britain.

St Albans Works FC, 1940. This is a wartime photograph and it is likely that these young men were apprentices or in reserved occupations, with skills that were important to the local community and to assist the enduring war effort.

Cyclists outside the Cross Keys pub, London Road, c. 1916. Cycling was a popular pastime during the early part of the twentieth century. In the days before the common ownership of cars, the bicycle offered an affordable means of exploring the open countryside. Many pubs advertised teas for cyclists.

Eleven

Events

The St Albans pageant, 1907. The St Albans pageant involved more than 2,000 performers. Here dignitaries pass from Chequer Street into High Street in procession to Verulamium Park. The eight episodes of the pageant were performed six times in front of audiences totalling more than 20,000. Although professionally directed the majority of performers, costume makers and organizers were volunteers.

Pageant procession, George Street, 1907. Performers make their way down George Street hill to the park.

Pageant House, 1907. This disused hat factory on the corner of Upper Marlborough Road and Victoria Street was made available to the 1907 Pageant Committee, by the city council, for use as an administrative headquarters. Every window and pillar carries an advert for the pageant.

Pageant soldiers, 1907. These performers, looking more like sea monsters from an episode of *Dr Who* than medieval soldiers, clearly took their roles very seriously.

St Albans Mummers' play, c. 1980. Father Christmas creates space for St George to celebrate his defeat of the dragon by challenging an opponent to a knockabout combat, the defeated victim being resurrected by a comic doctor. The traditional fool's costume is covered in strips of cloth. Mummers' plays are usually performed around the winter solstice, and celebrate the earth's reawakening.

Fireman's procession, *c.* 1910. This procession of horse-drawn fire appliances in Market Place seems rather too extensive for St Albans alone. It was almost certainly an inter-brigade contest and St Albans' turn to host the event.

Fireman's funeral, *c.* 1930. In this tribute to a dead colleague, a fire engine carries the coffin of an unfortunate fireman through the Peahen Junction at the top of Holywell Hill. This junction was at one time the busiest in the country and the first to have traffic lights, triggered by pressure pads, installed.

Beating the bounds, c. 1913. The ancient ceremony of beating the bounds involved Church of England parish congregations, led by the clergy and choir, walking round the boundaries of the parish beating the walls and hedges with sticks, seeing if repairs were needed. The modern version is led by the mayor and traces the four-mile long medieval boundary of the city.

Opening of the Redbourn bypass, 1984. A much needed bypass for Redbourn was opened on 29 October 1984. This modern convenience was marked by the passage of a stagecoach representing an important aspect of busy roads in past times.

Hospital fund raising procession, c. 1900. Cash shortages in hospitals are nothing new. This procession passing the Crystal Palace public house in London Road seems to be popular, judging by the crowds gathered along the route.

Travelling fair, Harpenden, c. 1900. Small, simple fairs such as this were very popular in less cynical and materialistic times. Half a dozen sideshows and two ranks of swings seem to be enough for the public to be entertained and for a sizeable group of travellers to make a living.

Jarrow march, St Peter's Street, 1936. The Jarrow march passed through St Albans on 29 October 1936. They are seen here leaving Stonecross at the northern end of St Peter's Street. The marchers were given a formal welcome by the mayor and provided with food, entertainment and places to rest overnight.

Andrew Carnegie, 1911. The American philanthropist donated money for the construction of public libraries; and St Albans benefited with a library built at the city end of Victoria Street. Granted the freedom of the city in recognition of his generosity, white bearded Carnegie stands next to the American flag.

Welcome home, c. 1902. A soldier is given a welcome when he returns home from the Boer War. The pub is the Black Lion in Fishpool Street.

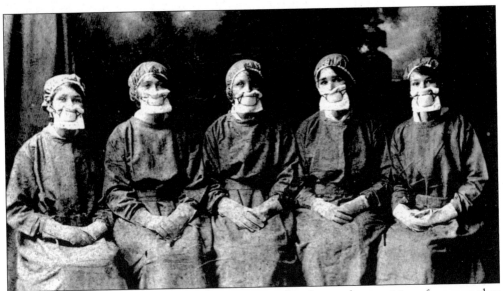

Munitions workers, c. 1916. These ladies were employed to make munitions for a war that consumed them at a frightening rate. Their overalls include face masks and rubber gloves, providing a little protection from the gunpowder they handled. Eleanor Button, who lived in Gustard Wood, can be seen second left. She travelled on foot and by train to the factory in Chorleywood.

Lt James McRobert and his family at London Colney airfield in 1919. He is seated in his SE5A aircraft with his wife and new-born son, Kenneth, alongside. McRobert was posted to London Colney in March 1918 after gaining his pilot's certificate the previous month. In February 1919 he was involved in an accident at London Colney when he collided with another aircraft while gliding into the aerodrome. He was not seriously injured.

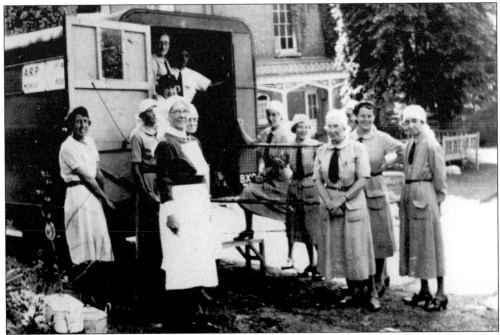

Second World War nurses, air-raid precautions van, c. 1942. Many women contributed to the war effort by working on the Home Front – in factories, with the WVS (Women's Voluntary Service), the WLA (Women's Land Army) and in civil defence.

Second World War soldiers, c. 1944. Men tended to be drafted into the fighting front. Frank Davies (centre) was a St Albans shoemaker in civilian life but found himself manning a 37mm mobile field gun in the Second World War.

VE Day street party, 1945. Victory in Europe Day saw many street parties, primarily for the children, but enjoyed by adults as well. Many of the adults gave up precious rations to make sure that the children had their treats. Here, the residents of Sopwell Lane and Bardwell Road celebrate.

Pre-fabs, 1950. Many people were made homeless by the war and the pre-fabricated house was the short-term solution to that problem. They were assembled on site, from factory made parts; often by supervised prisoners of war. The houses were designed to last for around twenty years but many have survived into the twenty-first century. Some prefabs survive in Mitchell Close.

Shop in French Row, 1951. John Boulting was making a film, called *The Magic Box*, to celebrate the achievements of film pioneer Willam Friese-Greene. He needed a doorway to represent the entrance to Friese-Greene's shop and chose Violet Wedge's old shop in French Row. It appears only for a few brief seconds as the star, Robert Donat, runs out of the door.

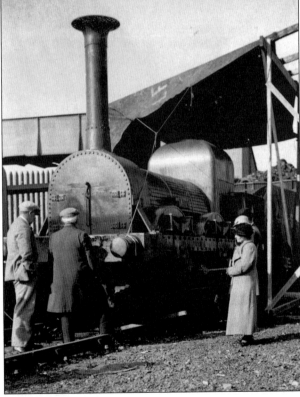

The *Lion* locomotive, *c.* 1937. Bricket Wood station doubled as the early Euston station for filming of *Queen Victoria* in 1937. The *Lion* locomotive was removed from its plinth in Liverpool Lime Street station and transported to Bricket Wood. Two 1840s coaches of the Liverpool and Manchester Railway were also borrowed. These later became part of the National Railway Museum collection in York.

Twelve
Religion

Aerial view of the abbey from the south, *c.* 1950. Founded in around 793 it was, until the Reformation, the premier Benedictine abbey in the country. The Deanery, to the right of the photograph, was the setting for the popular 1960s television series *All Gas and Gaiters*.

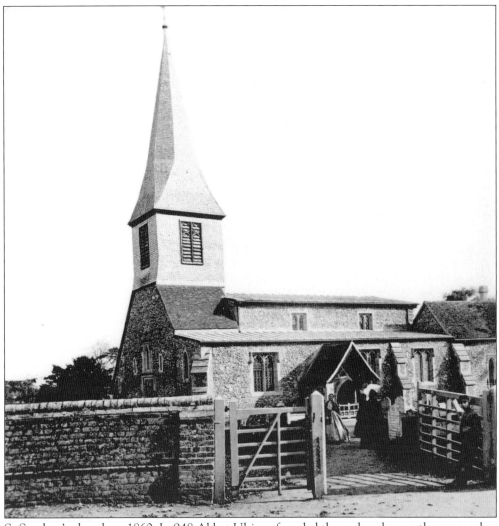

St Stephen's church, c. 1860. In 948 Abbot Ulsinus founded three churches on the approaches to St Albans – St Peter's, St Stephen's and St Michael's. St Stephen's is on the southern approach to the city and looks much the same today. The ladies are all wearing crinolines.

St Peter's church, c. 1885. This church, on the northern approach to St Albans, is the most central of the three churches. Here we see how it looked prior to its restoration, by Lord Grimthorpe, in the 1890s. A good view of St Peter's Green and the circular water pump and lamp can also be seen.

Aerial view of St Michael's church and village, c. 1945. St Michael's church was also restored by Lord Grimthorpe in the 1890s. Directly above the church is Verulamium Museum which opened in 1939. A mass of trees is on what is now the car park. Two allotment sites, used during the Second World War, are also visible.

Main entrance to All Saints Convent, London Colney, c. 1900. The All Saints Sisters of the Poor acquired Colney Park in 1897 and this building, with a stone sculptured frieze above the front door, was constructed shortly after. Since 1973 All Saints has been a pastoral centre for the Roman Catholic diocese of Westminster; the largest of its kind in the country.

Wesleyan church, Marlborough Road, c. 1900. This church was opened in 1898 to replace a chapel in Upper Dagnall Street which was no longer big enough. The church looks much the same today apart from the spire which was removed in 1970 because of loose tiles which were falling off the roof into the road below.

Christ Church, Verulam Road, *c.* 1910. Originally intended as a Roman Catholic church, Christ Church eventually opened as an Anglican church following the intervention – in 1857 – of Isabella Worley, a wealthy widow, who paid for its completion. Christ Church closed in 1974 and is now offices.

The west front of St Albans Abbey, *c*. 1860s. By the mid-nineteenth century the abbey was in a terrible state of repair. This view of the west front gives some idea of just how bad it had got before the restoration of the 1870s and 1880s. Lord Grimthorpe, who funded the restoration, is widely criticized for completely redesigning the abbey instead of just restoring it.

St Albans Abbey from the south-west, c. 1870. This Alpha postcard shows how the new abbey looked before Grimthorpe's restoration. The little house on the south-west corner of the abbey is on the site of the Abbot's house.

Abbey from the north-west, c. 1900. The abbey was completely transformed after Grimthorpe's work. Among many other changes, he added a pitched roof and a whole new façade to the west front. His changes caused a massive public outcry.

Faces on the south nave wall, *c.* 1950. Many of the faces have since been restored and a likeness of the face of the late Rt Revd Lord Robert Runcie was added in around 1980.

Treating the watching loft, *c.* 1930. The wooden watching loft where monks kept a constant vigil stands to the left of the shrine of St Alban as you look towards the Lady Chapel. Here the woodwork on the back of the loft is being sprayed with chemicals to guard against woodworm.

Working in the abbey roof space, 1930. Local builders, Miskins, were contracted to repair the vaulting above the presbytery ceiling. The timbers were also sprayed against death-watch beetle. A carpenter's mark (VIII) is just visible on the top right timber.

Treating the watching loft, c. 1930. An enormous wooden step ladder was used to ensure every inch of the intricately carved loft was treated against woodworm. The shrine of St Amphibalus is to the left of this photograph.

Cottages in the snow, Romeland, during the 1920s. Part of the west front of the abbey can be seen rising above the cottages. Romeland is the site of the martyrdom of George Tankerfield, a Protestant burned at the stake in 1555.

Wedding at St Paul's church, Hatfield Road, 1950s. A bride and her bridesmaids pose for a photograph before entering the church. St Paul's is on the corner of Blandford Road and the St Albans Co-operative Society grocer's shop can be seen on the opposite corner.

Bishops arriving at the Abbey, 1970. This Alf Gentle slide shows an informal moment during the enthronement of the Rt Revd Robert Runcie as Bishop of St Albans. The event involved civic dignitaries as well as officials from churches of all denominations. Runcie was Archbishop of Canterbury from 1980 to 1991. He died in St Albans in July 2000.

Interior of abbey, 1973. This very unusual view of the inside of the abbey was taken by Alf Gentle. Unfortunately, we do not know the occasion. All the furniture, fixtures and fittings have been removed, perhaps to make way for a major crafts exhibition.

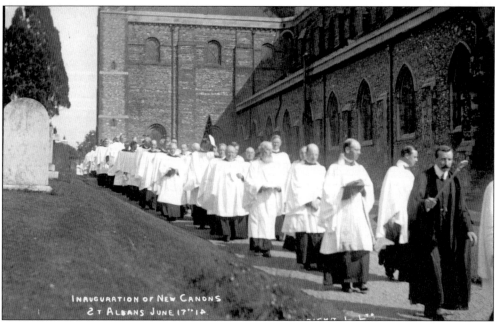

INAUGURATION OF NEW CANONS
ST ALBANS JUNE 17" 19

Inauguration of canons, St Albans Abbey, 1941. Clergy from throughout the Diocese of St Albans process to the abbey for the inauguration of new canons during the Second World War. The man in black, to the right, is Mr Abson, the verger.

Thirteen

Alf Gentle

Tunnel, St Peter's Street, 1969. There are many stories about tunnels under St Albans. This one is located under St Peter's Street near the church and was revealed when a foul drain collapsed. The rails and the truck suggest this is a long tunnel.

Skating, Verulamium Park, 1967. When the Verulamium lakes freeze over it is not long before winter sports enthusiasts appear.

Magna Carta procession, 1968. The procession was organized under the auspices of The Magna Carta Trust, formed to commemorate the grant of the Magna Carta. The first draft of the Magna Carta was produced in St Albans in 1213. In the centre of the picture is the be-wigged figure of Lord Denning (Master of the Rolls), the trust's chairman.

Lorry crash, Holywell Hill, *c.* 1958. This brick lorry crashed into the Crown and Anchor pub at the junction of Sopwell Lane and Holywell Hill. It is said, that despite the damage, the publican kept on serving!

Gentle's yard from the clock tower, 1971. This area has a long history and was once occupied by a number of separate yards stretching from French Row to Dagnall Street. The camper van, just right of centre in this photograph, was the home of Ginger Mills a well-known St Albans character. The back of Mrs Wedge's shop is also visible.

Installing the weather vane on the clock tower, 1971. Bob Peck, a local blacksmith, stands proudly next to the weather vane he had refurbished. Neither he nor his lady companion seems disturbed by their precarious position at the very tip of the tower.

Clock tower, 1965. This view of the clock tower is seen from the site of the old Dog and Christopher yards. They were both incorporated into Gentle's yard which itself became the site for Christopher Place.

St Albans factories, 1967. The building on the right is the Heath and Heather health food warehouse run by James Ryder, brother of Sam Ryder of Ryder Cup fame. Next to it is the smaller Roses Lime Juice factory and on the left, the offices of their parent company Schweppes. This building was once Lees' Shoe factory.

Sander's nursery, Camp Road, 1968. Demolition of an old railway bridge provides a view of the abandoned Sander's Orchid Nursery. Sander was known as the Orchid King and once provided a home to the largest orchid ever found. The *Cattleya Skinnerii* from Costa Rica was 7ft in diameter, 6ft high and in full bloom held 1,500 blossoms.

Green's department store, Chequer Street, 1969. This photograph is a nostalgic favourite with many who view the Alf Gentle collection. It shows the final day of Green's, a popular department store, closed because of the huge cost of modifications demanded by new fire regulations.

Work and play, c. 1970. Alf Gentle's hobby was photography, but his business was engineering. This mobile circular saw was one of his products.

Fourteen

Arthur
Melbourne-Cooper

Arthur Melbourne-Cooper and his daughter Audrey Wadowska, c. 1955. Arthur Melbourne-Cooper (1874-1961) was an important film pioneer who lived in St Albans. During the 1960s and 1970s Audrey campaigned tirelessly to get her father's work recognized. She died in 1982 aged seventy-two.

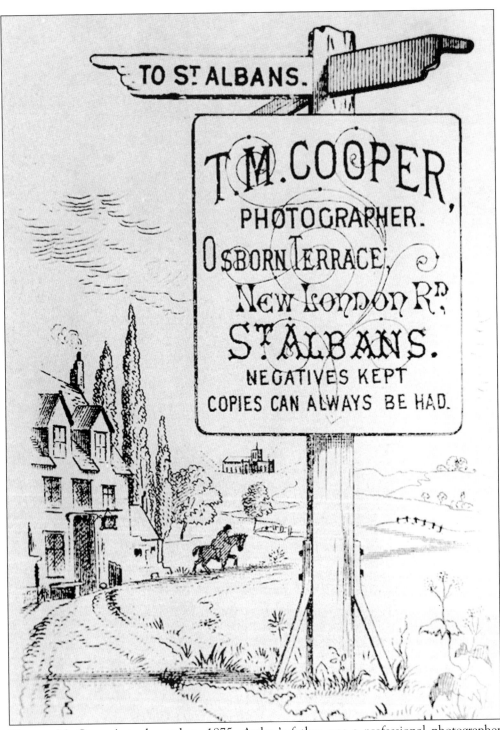

Thomas M. Cooper's trade card, *c.* 1875. Arthur's father was a professional photographer operating in St Albans from around 1860 until his death in 1901. His premises were at Osborn Terrace (No. 99 London Road). As a child Arthur helped his father in the studio, fostering a lifelong interest in photography and film.

George Hewitt, first chocolate-boy at the Alpha Picture Palace, *c.* 1910. In 1908 Arthur opened the Alpha Picture Palace on London Road. The cinema was a luxurious venue and the first in the country to offer plush, raked seating. Although the cinema was a great success, Melbourne-Cooper sold the cinema in 1911 because of financial difficulties.

Fire at the Regent cinema, 1927. In 1918 the Alpha Picture Palace re-opened as the Poly. It became the Regent in 1926 and was burnt down in December 1927. A new cinema was built on the site and this opened as the Capitol in 1931. It operated as the Odeon from 1945 until it closed in 1995.

The Bull Inn, London Colney, *c.* 1900. As well as making films and managing cinemas Arthur Melbourne-Cooper's Alpha Trading Company also produced picture postcards of local scenes. The Bull Inn stood on the main road between Barnet and St Albans and offered good stabling, quoits and skittles, as well as Christie's sparkling ales.

Dear's Temperance hotel, Nos 20-22 London Road, *c.* 1905. The Temperance Movement was very active during the Victorian and Edwardian periods and there are seven temperance organizations listed in the 1900 *St Albans Directory*. For several years Miss Dear was the treasurer of the British Women's Temperance Association which welcomed 'any woman or girl over fourteen years of age who is a total abstainer'.

Market Place in the snow, *c.* 1905. This Arthur Melbourne-Cooper photograph was, as far as we know, never made into a postcard. The snow appears fairly deep on the road but has been carefully cleared away from the pavement near the corn exchange.

THE WHITE HORSE, LONDON COLNEY (near St. Albans).   *Alpha, St. Albans.*

The White Horse, High Street, London Colney, *c.* 1905. Now renamed the Pear and Partridge, this pub has a history dating back to 1750. A horse trough is prominently positioned at the front of the building, close to the road.

Still from *Dream of Toyland*, 1907. This is one of Melbourne-Cooper's best known films and tells the story of a group of toys which come to life. The opening sequences were shot in St Peter's Street and from then on the film uses studio-based animation. From this still you can see that one of the shops has been given the name 'Collier' perhaps after Arthur's friend Stan Collier.

126

Still from *The Motor Pirate*, 1908. Like most of Melbourne-Cooper's films, *The Motor Pirate* was shot locally and can be regarded as one of the first science fiction films. Here we see the star of the show crossing the ford at Colney Heath. Comparison with the postcard below clearly identifies the local scene.

The ford at Colney Heath, *c.* 1910. The ford, road, cottages and houses are clearly identical to those in the film. The only real difference is in the trees – suggesting that this photograph was taken in the winter and the film was made in the summer.

Acknowledgements

We gratefully acknowledge the help of many people in this book. In particular, we would like to thank all those people, of which there are far too many to name individually, who have contributed photographs to the collections of St Albans Museums over the years. Without the generosity of these people, St Albans Museums would not have such excellent photographic collections providing such a good record of St Albans' past.

Special thanks are due to Chris Wilkinson, keeper of the Arthur Melbourne-Cooper archive, and Marjory Gentle for the donation of the Alf Gentle collection.

We are also grateful to our colleagues at St Albans Museums for their support, and especially to Jennifer Golding for scanning all the images in this book. Thanks also go to David Bolton, Barry Brooker, David Broom, Bill and Allana Clare, Frank Davies, Nancy Hale, Phil Hart, Eileen Hedges, The Hon. Henry Holland-Hibbert, Elizabeth Gardner, David Kelsall, Ethel and Cyril Martin, Pauline Roach, Roger Shepherd, Jeff Smyth, St Albans High School for Girls, Mark Suggitt, Dave Thorold, Gwen Tominey, Welwyn Hatfield Museums service, Matthew Wheeler, Orla Wheeler, Louise Wilkinson, Meriol Wilkinson, Geoff Woodward.